JESSE
VENTURA
TELLS IT LIKE IT IS

JESSE VENTURA

TELLS IT LIKE IT IS

AMERICA'S MOST OUTSPOKEN GOVERNOR SPEAKS OUT ABOUT GOVERNMENT

JESSE VENTURA
WITH **HERÓN MÁRQUEZ**

Lerner Publications Company

To the success of
third parties
everywhere   —jv

Lerner Publications Company
A division of Lerner Publishing Group
241 First Avenue North
Minneapolis, MN 55401 U.S.A.

Website address: www.lernerbooks.com

Library of Congress Cataloging-in-Publication Data

Ventura, Jesse.
   Jesse Ventura tells it like it is : America's most outspoken governor speaks out about
government / by Jesse Ventura ; with Herón Márquez.
      p.   cm.
Includes bibliographical references and index.
   ISBN 0-8225-0385-9 (lib. bdg. : alk. paper)
   1. United States—Politics and government—1993-2001—Juvenile literature. 2. Ventura,
Jesse—Juvenile literature. 3. Governors—Minnesota—Biography—Juvenile literature. 4.
Minnesota—Politics and government—1951—Juvenile literature. [1. United States—Politics
and government.] I. Márquez, Herón. II. Title.
   JK271.J464   2002
   977.6'053'092—dc21   2001006822

Manufactured in the United States of America
2 3 4 5 6 7—JR—07 06 05 04 03 02

CONTENTS

INTROD

BEFORE I WAS ELECTED GOVERNOR of Minnesota in 1998, wrestling fans around the country knew me as Jesse "The Body" Ventura. Football fans knew me as the voice of the Tampa Bay Buccaneers and the Minnesota Vikings. Movie fans might've seen me in the Arnold Schwarzenegger films *Predator* and *The Running Man*. A lot of Minnesotans also knew me as a loud, tell-it-like-it-is radio talk show host with opinions on everything, including politics. I guess winning the 1998 election surprised a lot of people, but not me. I never went into the election to lose. I always felt that, if the chips fell the right way, I could win.

My victory was such a long shot, though, it immediately got people's attention. All of a sudden, I became an influential U.S. politician. I got invited to the White House. Candidates for president came to visit me and asked for my support. And the Democratic and Republican Parties, the two dominant political

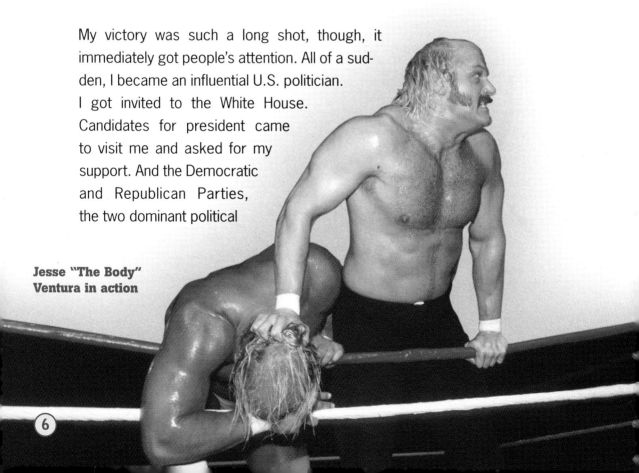

Jesse "The Body" Ventura in action

UCTION

groups, both tried to figure out what I'd done, because I'd defeated both their candidates.

That was kind of impossible, because I don't consider myself a politician. I don't act like one, talk like one, or dress like one. Yet, in 1990, I decided to run for mayor of Brooklyn Park, a large suburb of Minneapolis. I didn't run for office because I wanted to be the boss of everything but because I got angry with the politicians who controlled my town.

While campaigning for governor of Minnesota, Jesse Ventura set a new style by often wearing comfortable jeans—as well as ball caps, shirts, and jackets that advertised his favorite teams and causes.

At the time, my family and I were living in a house by the Mississippi River. We loved the peace and quiet of the river wetland. But a developer bought some vacant lots near us to build new homes. The developer's plans called for a subdivision neighborhood with curbs, gutters, sidewalks, and sewers. He wanted me and my neighbors to pay for these same things on our homes, so they would make his development more attractive. The city officials who ran Brooklyn Park agreed. The politicians thought the improvements would increase the value of the land, which would increase the property taxes paid by the owners.

> "I WALKED OUT OF THE MEETING KNOWING I WAS GOING TO RUN BECAUSE I SAW A MAYOR AND A COUNCIL THAT DIDN'T LISTEN TO THE PEOPLE THEY WERE ELECTED TO SERVE."

We—me and my neighbors—didn't think it was fair that we should have to pay for something we didn't want and didn't need. We were worried about what the development would do to the birds, the water, and the quality of life in the area. We were especially upset that putting in curbs, gutters, and a sewer system would mean having to remove dozens of trees from the wetland. So we let our representatives know.

About 450 of us signed a petition and took it to a city council meeting. The petition asked the city council members not to approve the development. We thought they'd listen to our concerns. After all, we'd elected these officials, and our taxes paid their salaries. Well, we were wrong. Our group was voted down 7–0 at what became an angry meeting.

I remember that the politicians didn't take us seriously. They told me the only way the development would stop was if there was a different mayor or city council. I threatened

JESSE VENTURA
MAYOR

CRAIG R.
CITY MANA

to run for office to make that happen, but they laughed at me, told me I couldn't win. I walked out of the meeting knowing I was going to run because I saw a mayor and a council that didn't listen to the people they were elected to serve.

Although I got involved in city politics for personal reasons, I quickly realized Brooklyn Park had a lot of people who felt just like I did. The city's politicians weren't listening to their concerns either. So I listened. My supporters and I also knocked on nearly every door in the city, and we explained to people why I was running. I didn't change my personality. I was still loud, still opinionated, still the same person they heard on the radio.

Later on, political observers were impressed not only by the fact that I won, but also by how I won. I beat the incumbent mayor, James Krautkremer, by more than 5,300 votes, and I beat him in every precinct, or voting area, of the city. Although the city then had about 55,000 residents, only about 2,500 people usually voted. But when I ran, more than 20,000 people voted.

The turnout proved to me that voters would get involved in politics again if someone was willing to take the time to talk straight to them and to really listen to their concerns.

Despite a few controversies over my style and dress, I think I did some good things for Brooklyn Park. I pushed to hire more police and got officers to patrol more effectively. The result was a drop in crime. I tried to help the city's economy by using what celebrity status I had to get more people to be aware of Brooklyn Park, a move that attracted businesses and visitors to the city. Eventually, though, I decided not to seek another term. I went back to my radio job, and I kept commenting on politics.

Meanwhile, in 1997, the state announced that it had a $4 billion surplus. This meant the government had taken in a lot more money in taxes than it needed. Hey, good news, I thought. I assumed the money would be returned to the taxpayers. I was wrong. Instead of returning the money, the state planned on finding some government programs to spend it on. I got angry again.

The more I brought up how unfair it was for the government to take in more money than it needed, the more callers started telling me how right I was. I told anyone who would listen that I was so mad I just might run for governor. If I won, I promised to give any government surplus back to the taxpayers.

Of course, the idea of me running for governor drew some laughs from politicians and journalists around the state. They figured it was one thing to be a suburban mayor but quite another to be the governor of a state. Except, I wasn't kidding. What's more, I predicted I'd win. I was pretty sure people weren't excited about the two candidates who were running (the Republican, Norm Coleman, and the Democrat, Skip Humphrey). They were boring. People were tired of business as usual when it came to politics. Voters were looking for something different. People began calling my radio show to say they would volunteer to help my campaign. I took their support seriously. I didn't make a joke out of it.

What voters were looking for was an alternative to the Republicans and the Democrats. I'm an independent thinker, so I ran as a third-party independent candidate. Pretty much all a third-party candidate has to do to win is convince enough people—Republicans, Democrats, and independents—to vote for him or her. Persuading people is what I'm good at. I speak my mind and tell people the truth. People respect straight talk, even if it's not what they want to hear.

The Jesse Ventura air freshener

WHO CAN VOTE?

Some voting requirements, such as length of residence, vary from state to state. But, in general, any U.S. citizen who is eighteen years of age or older can register to vote. In most cases, a driver's license, a passport, or a birth certificate provides the needed information. I know voting is a hard sell. What do you think kids would rather do, go to the Ozzfest or vote? Now, if you had Ozzy Osbourne at the voting booth, then you might get a big turnout. I think someday you'll be able to vote on the Internet, and that'll help turnout.

Until then, on Election Day, the voter goes to a polling place, usually at a school or other large building. He or she is given a ballot, or list of the candidates, and then is directed into a private booth, where the ballot is marked, indicating which of the candidates gets a vote.

I always tell people to vote your heart and your conscience. Don't go in and vote like you're out at the racetrack trying to pick a winner. Choose whomever you think is the best. Too often people vote to be on the winning side, and that to me is wasting your vote.

After the ballots are collected, they are counted and taken or sent electronically to the local election board or elections clerk to be certified, or OK'd. The winner is announced, usually by the next day—although a lot of newspaper and television journalists like to tell people ahead of time who they think will be the likely winner. I know it's free speech, but I think projecting winners should be banned. I don't think the media should be able to put up those check marks. There should be a national law that says every polling place must be closed before winners can be announced. If you're in California and you get off work in the evening and the news already declared who's the president, why would you vote?

A voter signs in at her polling place and gets her ballot.

On victory night in 1998, a young man *(left)* happily hoists a Ventura for Governor sign, while the new governor-elect *(below)* shouts his approval of the voting results.

As the campaign wore on, I could tell people were listening to me. But the polls, which show how popular candidates are, said I was far behind. But polltakers usually talk only to registered voters (those who formally sign up to vote). I knew I was making a big impression on two other groups—people who had given up on voting and so were no longer registered and people who had never voted before. The people in those two groups liked what I was saying, and I was convincing them to register to vote for me. I was especially good at getting college students and other young people to vote for the first time.

So on election night, my victory did indeed shock the world. Almost immediately, people began wondering how and why I'd won. Journalists and politicians said my election might be a turning point in the history of U.S. politics. Just as quickly, people started wondering if I'd take the lead of the third-party movement. I figured that if an independent could win in Minnesota, there was no reason an independent couldn't win in other states or even in a national election.

1 WHAT GOVERN

OK, THAT'S THE STORY about how I got into the business of governing. But let's talk about what government actually is. At times, it scares people, because it's so big. Not only are there various levels of government (federal, state, and local), but there are also thousands of agencies and departments within those levels of government. They make laws that affect just about everything in our lives.

A long time ago, though, way back at the beginning of human history, there was no United States and no government of any sort. For thousands of years, people lived without governments telling them what to do. No one was telling parents they had to send their children to school. In fact, there were no schools.

While that might sound great to some people (especially some kids), in reality I think things were pretty wild. Without any rules, people settled their arguments with fists, clubs, rocks, sticks, or other crude weapons. The world probably felt like a big playground where the bullies ruled. Without government, no one was protecting people or catching criminals.

If things had kept going this way, it would've been pretty hard for people to build homes, farms, roads, businesses, and cities. Luckily, some of the smarter people stopped fighting long enough to form groups to protect themselves against the bullies. The first groups were probably extended families. These groups had a few basic rules, like

A painting from a cave in what would later become the African nation of Zimbabwe. Such ancient artworks help us understand how early humans lived.

IS MENT

don't steal from one another and don't hurt one another. But they didn't really have a government, because there wasn't much discussion about who would make decisions and who would enforce the rules.

Thousands of years ago, folks figured out that if family groups were good, then bigger groups would be even better. Larger groups would provide better protection from the world's dangers. So family groups joined together to form larger groups called tribes or clans.

The families in a tribe usually had something in common with each other. They either spoke the same language, or lived in the same general area, or maybe they just all looked alike. Tribes provided better protection from bullies, and they also forced people to start working together to improve their lives. Jobs were divided, and everyone had a job to do to help the

tribe. People also had to cooperate with one another to make decisions for the group. This was probably the true start of government.

The path toward a government we'd recognize probably began when tribal members formally chose a leader to

make the important decisions for them. Eventually, tribal leadership proved so successful that villages and later towns were founded. From these beginnings came the first informal governments. People decided as a group what was right, what was wrong, what was important, or what was needed. The group identified goals—such as providing enough food or strengthening defenses—and established punishments for breaking the rules.

From these informal governments come the complicated systems that now govern us. At the heart of our government is a basic agreement among people to live together, to obey the laws of the society, and to accept punishment for breaking the laws. Not everyone agrees to this, of course. There are still modern-day bullies, such as the terrorists who attacked the World Trade Center and the Pentagon. But most people believe it's better to agree to disagree rather than to resort to violence.

BASIC FORMS OF GOVERNMENT

Democracies and republics, in which the citizens elect their own representatives, are the most common forms of government these days. In these types of governments, things are decided by majority votes, but the rights of minorities are respected.

At the other extreme are absolute monarchies, which are countries run only by kings or queens, who have inherited the position and who have unlimited power. Saudi Arabia has an absolute monarchy. Britain has a limited monarchy in which the hereditary king or queen has only some, mostly ceremonial, power. Monarchies have probably been around longer than any other formal form of government. The pharaohs who ruled Egypt for thousands of years were kings or queens, with their sons or daughters taking over simply because they were part of the royal family.

Under a dictatorship, all power is held by one person. Usually dictators are or were military people who took over a nation's government by force. They generally hold on to power by using (or threatening to use) military might against their own citizens. Saddam Hussein of Iraq is an example of a modern-day military dictator.

A fairly new form of government called Communism came into being in the twentieth century. Communism was inspired by the writings of the nineteenth-century German economist Karl Marx. Under a Communist system, everyone is supposed to be equal, and there is no private property. Everything is owned by the state for the benefit of everyone in the state. There's only one problem. This system requires people to be perfect. In reality, Communist governments came to be more like dictatorships, and many of them, including the former Soviet Union, collapsed in the early 1990s.

The statue of Pharaoh Ramses II in Egypt

2) FREE CONSTI

LET'S TAKE A LOOK BACK at our country's beginnings. How else are you gonna learn what's important? Until 1776 the United States wasn't a nation at all. It was a bunch of separate territories and colonies, or overseas possessions, of European nations. The most organized group was the thirteen British colonies along the East Coast. Britain was a monarchy ruled by a king and the British Parliament. Rules set by Parliament and in the name of the British monarch governed the thirteen colonies.

In 1776 leading American colonists decided the colonies should break away from British rule. They signed the Declaration of Independence to tell the king just what they had in mind. The Revolutionary War (1775–1783) was fought, in part, because the colonists didn't want to live under the British monarchy. They wanted to elect their own leaders, to set their own tax rates, and to decide things for themselves.

After the Americans defeated the British in 1783, the next job for these leaders—we've nicknamed them the Founding Fathers—was to write a document that spelled

The constitutional delegates asked George Washington *(standing, holding paper)* to run the convention in Philadelphia in 1787. His calming presence kept the delegates focused on their goal—to write the Constitution.

DOM AND THE TUTION

out exactly how the United States of America was to operate. They also wanted to write something that would correct the wrongs they saw in the British system. So fifty-five of the Founding Fathers, all white men, all land-holders, arrived in Philadelphia, Pennsylvania, in May of 1787, to attend the Constitutional Convention.

Their job was to draft a document that would create a new political system. The delegates decided to hold the convention in secret, with the doors and windows closed, so no one outside could hear what was being said inside. The Founding Fathers wanted to create a new type of government, and they wanted to be able to speak their minds freely. The document they wrote was the U.S. Constitution.

Because of their experience with the British king, the Founding Fathers were afraid to give their new government too much power. They didn't want to create a new kingdom in America. Believe it or not, the delegates to the Constitutional Convention viewed government as a necessary evil.

The Founding Fathers knew they wanted a republic, or representative system, in which the citizens of the country would decide how to run things. Right from the start, in the first paragraph of the Constitution, in fact, the Founding Fathers laid out their ultimate goal in what has come to be known as the preamble to the Constitution:

We the People of the United States, in Order to form a more perfect Union, establish Justice, insure domestic Tranquility, provide for the common defence, promote the general Welfare, and secure the Blessings of Liberty to ourselves and our Posterity, do ordain and establish this Constitution for the United States of America.

In almost five months of work, the Founding Fathers created a three-part system of government. They set up the executive branch, headed by the president, to lead the country and to enforce the laws. The legislative branch of elected representatives in Congress (the House of Representatives and the Senate) was set up to make the laws. The judicial branch, made up of justices and the courts, was set up to figure out what the laws mean.

Having three separate branches of government, each looking over the shoulder of the others, was a work of genius. It made the government as corruption proof as it could be, and it assured that one leader or one branch would not step on the rights of the others.

Although the Constitution created something pretty outstanding, the Founding Fathers realized it wasn't perfect. Some of them argued that the Constitution gave too much power to the federal government, and they wanted more limits. Others wanted protections guaranteed for individuals.

To take care of these concerns, the delegates added ten amendments, or changes, to the Constitution. These amendments, known as the Bill of Rights, set limits on the government's power and defined the rights and protections that citizens would enjoy. The Bill of Rights is only 462 words long, but those 462 words are probably the most important ever written in this country. In many ways, the Bill of Rights makes everyone equal in

The original version of the Bill of Rights

the eyes of the law, whether the person is the president of the United States or a chicken farmer on an Arkansas ranch.

In my view, the Bill of Rights protects people from too much government. It's in government's nature, in some ways, to want more and more power. And so having a set of rules that can't be broken makes a lot of sense. If government steps over that line, then it's no longer government of the people, by the people, and for the people. Still, the Founding Fathers knew that the world was a dangerous place, so they put certain powers in the Constitution to be used in extreme circumstances. The government can use these powers to protect itself and us in times of war or in other hazardous situations.

The Constitution and the Bill of Rights—which were meant to govern an expanding country—were based on a very simple idea: freedom. Freedom to vote. Freedom to choose. Freedom to worship. Freedom to move about. Freedom to speak your mind. Freedom to live as you wish. Freedom to do as much—or as little—with your life as you want to. The only real limitations on that freedom, in broad terms, are that you can't hurt someone or violate someone's freedom. If you did, that's where the government would step in, either to stop you from doing this or to punish you if you'd already hurt someone.

What exactly does the Bill of Rights say? The First Amendment, without a doubt in my view, is the most important. It gives people freedom of speech, or the right to say what's on their mind without worrying about being sent to jail or made to shut up. The First Amendment also gives people the constitutional right to hang out with whomever they want and to believe whatever they want without government interference. (How your parents may feel about these issues is another thing altogether.) Even if others don't like what you have to say, the First Amendment says that no government official or government agency can tell you to stop. The First Amendment also guards your freedom to believe in any religion you choose.

The Second Amendment says that people have a right to own guns, and the government can't pass a law prohibiting you from doing so. Again, that's there to protect you from too much government.

Protesters *(above)* show their opposition to handguns, while *(below)* supporters of the National Rifle Association (NRA) recruit new members. Both activities are protected by the Bill of Rights.

THE BILL OF RIGHTS

The first ten amendments to the Constitution are called the Bill of Rights. They outline not only what U.S. citizens can do but also what the U.S. government cannot do. The entire Bill of Rights, which is less than 500 words, was ratified, or agreed to, on December 15, 1791. The language is old-style English.

Amendment I

Congress shall make no law respecting an establishment of religion, or prohibiting the free exercise thereof; or abridging the freedom of speech, or of the press; or the right of the people peaceably to assemble, and to petition the Government for a redress of grievances.

Amendment II

A well-regulated Militia, being necessary to the security of a free State, the right of the people to keep and bear Arms shall not be infringed.

Amendment III

No Soldier shall, in time of peace be quartered in any house, without the consent of the Owner, nor in time of war, but in a manner to be prescribed by law.

Amendment IV

The right of the people to be secure in their persons, houses, papers, and effects, against unreasonable searches and seizures, shall not be violated, and no Warrants shall issue, but upon probable cause, supported by Oath or affirmation, and particularly describing the place to be searched, and the persons or things to be seized.

Amendment V

No person shall be held to answer for a capital, or otherwise infamous crime, unless on a presentment or indictment of a Grand Jury, except in cases arising in the land or naval forces, or in the Militia, when in actual service in time of War or public danger; nor shall any person be subject for the same offense to be twice put in jeopardy of life or limb; nor shall be compelled in any criminal case to be a witness against himself, nor be deprived of life, liberty, or property, without due process of law; nor shall private property be taken for public use, without just compensation.

Amendment VI

In all criminal prosecutions, the accused shall enjoy the right to a speedy and public trial, by an impartial jury of the State and district wherein the crime shall have been committed, which district shall have been previously ascertained by law, and to be informed of the nature and cause of the accusation; to be confronted with the witnesses against him; to have compulsory process for obtaining witnesses in his favor, and to have the Assistance of Counsel for his defence.

Amendment VII

In suits at common law, where the value in controversy shall exceed twenty dollars, the right of trial by jury shall be preserved, and no fact tried by a jury, shall be otherwise reexamined in any Court of the United States, than according to the rules of the common law.

James Madison, a delegate from Virginia, was almost single-handedly responsible for writing the Bill of Rights.

Amendment VIII

Excessive bail shall not be required, nor excessive fines imposed, nor cruel and unusual punishments inflicted.

Amendment IX

The enumeration in the Constitution, of certain rights, shall not be construed to deny or disparage others retained by the people.

Amendment X

The powers not delegated to the United States by the Constitution, nor prohibited by it to the States, are reserved to the States respectively, or to the people.

> "THE CONSTITUTION AND THE BILL OF RIGHTS . . . WERE BASED ON A VERY SIMPLE IDEA: FREEDOM."

The Third Amendment says homeowners can't be forced to house soldiers during times of peace. That's to prevent the military from occupying towns or cities in our own country.

The Fourth Amendment says that police officers and the courts must be strongly convinced there is evidence of a crime to justify searching you or your possessions. Without this safeguard, the police or a government agency could stop and search you or break into your home anytime they wanted. No one wants a police state, where the government has the power to determine your guilt or innocence without a fair trial, to fabricate evidence, or to unreasonably enter your home or take your things.

The Fifth Amendment is an interesting one. It says no one can make you confess to a crime. If you don't want to admit it or talk about it, you can remain silent. That's why, in a lot of the old Hollywood gangster movies, you will sometimes see the accused gangster "take the Fifth." This amendment prevents the government from obtaining confessions by force and makes the government prove its case.

Other amendments make sure that accused people have speedy trials, pay a fair bail after being arrested, and have fair fines and punishments. These amendments guarantee that government can't simply imprison you without a solid reason.

CHANGING THE CONSTITUTION

One of the reasons the Constitution has survived is that it can be amended, or changed, if needed. Usually the change comes about after someone challenges the legality or fairness of a law. The dispute may go to a local or state court, where a local or state judge decides. Eventually, if the case is important enough, it may end up in the U.S. Supreme Court. The Constitution made the U.S. Supreme Court the final word on all legal disputes.

If people aren't happy with what the U.S. Supreme Court has decided, they can try a different option. They can ask Congress to amend the Constitution, just as the Founding Fathers had done when adding the Bill of Rights.

The Constitution even spells out how an amendment can be added to the Constitution. The petition to ask for the change must be put forth by a member of Congress. The amendment must be passed by Congress and then must get two-thirds of the states of the Union to ratify it. Amendments to the Constitution have freed slaves, have given women suffrage (the right to vote), and have lowered the voting age from twenty-one to eighteen. All told, the Constitution has twenty-seven amendments, the last having been added in 1992.

An African American slave picks cotton in the early 1800s. After the Civil War (1861–1865), two different amendments addressed the civil rights of blacks. The Fourteenth Amendment set forth that every person born in the United States is a U.S. citizen. The Fifteenth Amendment guaranteed blacks the right to vote.

INTERNATIONAL VENTURA

I'm convinced that the Founding Fathers wanted each state to be as strong as it could possibly be. They decided the federal government would set up national defense, enforce the laws, and negotiate treaties. Apart from that, each state was free to do what it thought best to make itself and its citizens strong and successful.

One area I believe remains firmly in the grasp of the states is business and trade, especially with other countries. When the Constitution and the Bill of Rights were first created, the world was a much simpler place. International trade and business were conducted only by federal governments and very large companies that could afford to send ambassadors abroad. But the world seems to be shrinking because of jet planes, telephones, and the Internet. With these instruments, businesspeople in Japan, China, Mexico, and the United States can talk to one another easily and quickly. No one needs a big government to make connections abroad.

I've traveled abroad frequently to promote trade with Minnesota. During a trade mission to Mexico, I met with the new and the outgoing presidents of Mexico. I toured businesses, visited hospitals, and talked to people about doing business in Minnesota. I also talked about Minnesota companies and what they had to offer each country. I made the same points during trips to Japan and Canada.

I have to treat the state of Minnesota and its economy like we're our own country. I believe it's my role as a governor to look out for my state's economy and to make it as viable in the economic world as I can.

During his trade trip to Japan, Governor Ventura bows respectfully to a Shinto priest in front of a monument to great sumo wrestlers.

The Tenth Amendment reflects some of the concerns the Founding Fathers had with states' and individuals' rights. It says anything that isn't outlined in the Constitution is under the authority of state or local governments. Personally, I believe in strong states' rights. I'd like to see states be able to govern themselves on most issues.

Although the Founding Fathers had a simple plan for running the country (one person, one vote), the world grew more complex than they could have ever imagined. The Founding Fathers had Britain and a few European powers to worry about. But they didn't have to deal with cars, planes, nuclear bombs, terrorists, the Internet, spaceships, and dozens of television stations that transmit throughout the world. The country back then had a few million people, not millions and millions of people. Most of the people believed in the same general ideas.

Much of the writing of the Constitution is credited to Gouverneur Morris, a delegate from Pennsylvania. (By the way, in English, his first name isn't a job title, and he lost his leg in a carriage accident.)

Yet, for more than 200 years, the United States has survived and prospered. Many people believe that the Constitution and the Bill of Rights made this success possible. Not bad for what started out as a bunch of white guys sitting inside a sweaty Philadelphia meeting room.

THE MANY GOVER

GOVERNMENT CAN SEEM very mysterious and complicated. There are so many agencies, boards, and institutions working at so many different levels that it can often seem as if you are wandering around in a giant maze. Most people feel that we have to have a set of rules, or government, but government has grown to mammoth proportions, especially on the federal level.

"WITH ALL THE FLAWS OUR GOVERNMENT HAS, IN MY VIEW, THERE'S STILL NONE BETTER ANYWHERE IN THE WORLD."

Yet, despite the size of government, its basic structure is still pretty simple. A good way to look at the various levels of U.S. government is to think of them as a pyramid instead of as a maze. The pyramid is made up of three layers—local, state, and federal.

Local governments form the base of the pyramid. Local governments, like the one in Brooklyn Park, run cities, towns, or villages around the country. They are usually made up of a mayor, a city council, or a county board. Local governments aren't nearly as big as the federal and state governments, but they do similar things. They make local laws. They

It's standing room only at a town meeting in Elmore, Vermont, as citizens wait to discuss town business.

LEVELS OF NMENT

raise money both by taxing residents for property they own and by charging a sales tax. The money is used to run schools, maintain roads, and pay for police, firefighters, and other city workers.

I think it's important for people to pay attention to local government. It'll probably affect you more than the government in Washington, D.C., ever will. Local politicians make decisions that can directly and quickly affect your pocketbook, your taxes, and your lifestyle.

Above the local governments, forming the middle of the pyramid, are the fifty state governments. They are smaller versions of the federal government. Like the U.S. and local governments, state governments collect taxes, make laws, and run courts and prisons. State governments include the governor and the state legislature, which, in most cases, has elected representatives and senators from towns and cities all over the state. (Nebraska is the only state so far with a unicameral, or one-house, legislature.)

The governor is the state version of the president. He or she is elected to serve for a fixed number of years and is in charge of various agencies in the state. The state legislature is like the U.S. Congress and is charged with setting up budgets, or lists, saying how much will be spent and on what programs. It also proposes and passes laws. The top state court is that state's version of the Supreme Court.

At the top of the pyramid is the federal government. The federal government rules because the Constitution says so. That's why state governments generally must do what the federal government says, and local governments generally must follow the state governments. Although there is only one U.S. Congress, one U.S. Supreme Court, and one U.S. president, the federal government needs the most people to keep it operating. The U.S. Congress has the final word on changing or creating federal laws and paying federal taxes. The U.S. Supreme Court has the final word on federal legal disputes. And the U.S. president has the final word when it comes to enforcing those laws and to speaking for the United States with other countries.

The three federal branches provide a system of checks and balances. This system is designed to make each branch equal to the others and to prevent any one branch from becoming more powerful than the rest. I think they maintain the best balance you can get today. At the same time, the system is set up so it can react quickly to emergencies.

President George W. Bush addresses Congress during his first State of the Union address.

IN AN EMERGENCY

With all the levels of government we have in our system, you might think there'd be chaos during an emergency. The reality is the three main levels are set up to work together to get things done under the worst circumstances.

At the local level, government oversees the use of money in its budget to pay for local police and firefighters. In an emergency, local governments can ask for backup from state forces, such as the National Guard.

During a statewide disaster, the state government, through the state's governor, has the power to make aid available for emergency relief and cleanup. The governor can also direct the National Guard to help out local law enforcement. The Departments of Public Health and Public Safety may also get involved.

Much of the work at the state and local levels is mirrored at the federal level, where the Federal Emergency Management Agency (FEMA) is one of the major players. The federal government oversees national security, using several means at its disposal, including the national military, the Federal Bureau of Investigation (FBI), and the Central Intelligence Agency (CIA).

Let's take a look at a couple of examples from 2001—spring floods in Minnesota and the World Trade Center attacks in New York—and see how the levels worked together.

In April of 2001, spring rains caused massive flooding in my state. The Minnesota counties involved immediately organized cleanup crews and hired contractors to remove debris and fix houses. Meanwhile, I issued an executive order that authorized the State Emergency Operations Center to coordinate assistance to flooded areas. I further authorized the Division of Emergency Management to ask for federal assistance and ordered the National Guard to the area to protect people's lives and property. FEMA came in to assess the damage. Based on FEMA's recommendation, President Bush declared Minnesota a federal disaster area, a move that resulted in the immediate release of

Members of the Minnesota National Guard form a sandbag line during the floods of April 2001.

federal money to help pay for cleanup, repairs, and for emergency services.

In the case of flooding, governments typically have time to prepare. The terrorist attacks on the World Trade Center took everyone by surprise. Nevertheless, each level made sure its area of responsibility was covered. Within minutes, New York City police and firefighters were at the scene. Under the direction of Mayor Rudy Giuliani, the city's Department of Health responded within hours to set up medical services for the wounded. Other health agencies checked the air quality after the disaster.

Meanwhile, Governor George Pataki declared a state disaster, ordered in the National Guard to help with search and rescue, and authorized health services to bring in ambulance crews from around the state. He ordered the State Emergency Operations Center to coordinate assistance between agencies. He also asked President Bush to declare the area a federal disaster so that the state could qualify for federal money to help pay for relief and cleanup.

In his role as commander in chief, President Bush immediately put all U.S. military on high alert. The Federal Aviation Agency (FAA) temporarily grounded or

Firefighters and rescue workers at the World Trade Center site in September 2001

diverted all flights. FEMA sent in urban search-and-rescue teams, medical teams, and mortuary teams. Later, President Bush asked state governors to use their National Guards to ensure airport security until the federal government could take over that role. I was happy to oblige, and the Minnesota National Guard began patrolling our major airports.

Congress and the president together pushed through an aid package to provide health services, to relieve small businesses that had to close, and to pay the workers who were removing all the debris from the site. Less than one month after the attacks, the president also created the Office of Homeland Security, which is charged with coordinating and prioritizing all efforts to prepare for, respond to, and prevent terrorist attacks in the United States.

All in all, this country pulls together best when it's against the wall. The events of 2001 proved this beyond a doubt.

(Left) Major legal cases are tried before the nine-member court at the U.S. Supreme Court Building in Washington, D.C. No photography is allowed during the proceedings, so the news media typically show drawings of the justices, juries, and lawyers. (Below) The stairway to the U.S. Senate. The House of Representatives, the other part of Congress, has its own separate meeting place within the capitol.

The checks and balances are smart, especially when there's no national emergency. While Congress can make laws, it is up to the Supreme Court to decide if they are constitutional. While the president can decide to make

The cabinet *(shown at a press conference)* is made up of people who run most of the departments of the federal government. They meet with the president to discuss strategies, to review legislation, and to advise the president on international matters.

war on another country, Congress has to agree with the idea and to set aside the money needed to fight the war. And while the Supreme Court interprets the laws, the president appoints the justices of the Supreme Court, whom Congress has to OK before they can take office. With all the flaws our government has, in my view, there's still none better anywhere in the world.

WHAT DOES A PRESIDENT DO?

The Founding Fathers created the job of president of the United States in 1787. They didn't want to create an all-powerful king, so they made sure the president would be an equal partner with Congress and the Supreme Court.

So what exactly does the president do? The president of the United States carries out the laws that Congress makes. The president can veto, or stop, a bill (an idea for a law) from being passed by Congress by refusing to sign it.

The president is commander in chief of all the armed forces. It's this part of the job that President George W. Bush exercised in the fall of 2001, when he ordered ships, planes, and armed services personnel to their posts after the World Trade Center attacks.

The president is also responsible for naming judges to the U.S. Supreme Court. This means the president can try to appoint people who are more likely to agree with the president's ideas when deciding if a law or action is constitutional. Also, the president chooses the hundreds of federal judges around the country, something that only increases the president's influence on society and the country.

The president also selects all heads of federal agencies, such as the FBI, the CIA, and the Department of Agriculture. Some of the agency bosses belong to a group called the cabinet, which advises the president when the president needs to make important decisions. The president also names the U.S. ambassadors to other countries.

A U.S. Navy crew member services an F-14A Tomcat on the USS *Enterprise.* The carrier was ordered by President Bush to participate in the war against terrorism.

The Constitution says that each year the president must tell Congress and the rest of the country how things are going. The president usually makes this speech—called the State of the Union address—in January to a joint session of Congress

President Bush represented the United States in trade talks with Vicente Fox, the president of Mexico *(left)*, and Jean Chrétien, prime minister of Canada *(center)*.

(when members of the Senate and the House sit together as one group). The Congress also holds a joint session when the president reports on treaties negotiated with foreign countries. It would be confusing to have serious discussions if the United States spoke with many different voices. So the Constitution says the president is the one who speaks for the country when making treaties, agreements, or alliances with other countries. This part of the president's job also came into play in late 2001, when President Bush brought together other countries that wanted to fight terrorism.

Although the president enjoys tremendous power, the president's power isn't unlimited. The Constitution limits the president's term of office to four years and limits a president to two terms in office. The president has to be at least thirty-five years old, must be a natural-born citizen of the United States (not an immigrant), and must have lived in the country for at least fourteen years.

4 VOTING ELECTION

ALMOST EVERYONE IN MINNESOTA thought I was joking when I announced that I was going to run for governor. Although I was well known locally, I was at a great disadvantage because I didn't belong to either of the two major political parties. It seemed impossible to challenge them. The Democrats and the Republicans not only dominate politics in Minnesota but in each of the fifty states. In fact, in one form or another, the two parties have dominated the U.S. political process almost since our country was founded.

AND
CAMPAIGNS

I hadn't raised a lot of campaign money, which every political expert in the country believed was essential to succeed. In my view, if you're a Democrat or a Republican, money is the driving force of politics. You go out and you cover any of these major candidates, and I'll bet you dollars to doughnuts, five of every six days are spent on political fund-raising. But if the candidates are raising money, they aren't talking issues.

I knew my goal was difficult. A few months before the election, local newspapers ran stories showing that I was running a distant third in popularity polls among registered voters. They didn't pretend I didn't exist, they just didn't think I was a factor. They believed all the so-called experts.

> "I'LL BET YOU DOLLARS TO DOUGHNUTS, FIVE OF EVERY SIX DAYS ARE SPENT ON POLITICAL FUND-RAISING. BUT IF THE CANDIDATES ARE RAISING MONEY, THEY AREN'T TALKING ISSUES."

People paid $500 a ticket to attend a political fund-raising event in New York in 2001.

In winning against such long odds, I showed a lot of what was right—and what was wrong—with the election process in this country. On the plus side, the election victory proved that anybody can be elected to high office. Politically, in some ways, my election was a wake-up call—certainly in Minnesota if not in America—that the two major political parties aren't fulfilling everyone's vision. They don't share a lot of ground in what I call the commonsense middle.

Two things really helped me win the election. First, I told people exactly what I thought, regardless of what I thought they wanted to hear. I took the commonsense approach of speaking to them in a language they could understand. The other thing I did was to seek the support of the thousands of young voters in the state who either had never voted before or who had given up on voting. I knew from my Brooklyn Park experience that if I could reach kids, along with those voters who were fed up with the two major parties, I had a good chance. So I visited schools and went to areas of cities where young people hung out. I was the antiestablishment candidate. I identified with these kids, and I paid attention to them.

Older voters rallied to Ventura's gubernatorial campaign. Many of them had given up on voting but returned to the polling places in 1998.

RUNNING FOR OFFICE

Just because a person wants to run for a major office doesn't mean he or she can. Each state has its own requirements, and these vary from state to state. If a person wants to run as a Democratic or Republican candidate, for example, he or she will need to get that party's nomination. An independent, however, doesn't have to worry about being nominated. But a candidate typically has to get a certain number of registered voters in that state to support his or her intention of running for office. The voters show their support by signing a petition. In most states, a candidate also needs to apply to be on the ballot within a certain time frame before the election.

Ralph Nader was the Green Party's nominee in the 2000 presidential election. As a third-party candidate, Nader wasn't invited to the national debates with the candidates from the two major parties.

So you're on the ballot. Now what? Many factors determine whether a candidate will succeed in being elected. If you have a major party's endorsement, or support, you'll likely have access to money and staff to help you get elected. If you aren't associated with a major political party, you face a challenge. You'll need to raise money to let voters know about you and about your qualifications. You might need help with public relations, which also costs money. You also need to convince voters that their vote for a third-party candidate won't be wasted. I had to do this, but it's paid off. There's always that possibility now that a Democrat or a Republican might not win, and that's good. It shows people that your vote counts, and it makes the Democrats and the Republicans work harder to earn your vote.

ON POLITICAL PARTIES

In whatever I've done in my life, I've always considered myself a maverick, a person willing to do his own thing regardless of what others are doing or thinking. It's no wonder I'm an independent.

Because I don't belong to either party, I'm free to act like a Republican when I think it makes sense to and to act like a Democrat when it makes sense. I take what I like from Republicans (such as lower taxes) and from Democrats (liberal social policies).

Money, in fact, is the biggest complaint I have with the U.S. political process and with the Democrats and Republicans in particular. Money is at the heart of modern American politics because so much of it is needed to finance campaigns. It's not unusual for presidential candidates to spend about $100 million. When I ran for governor, I spent $600,000. My Republican and Democratic opponents combined spent $13 million.

I'd like to see term limits for politicians so that there can be turnover in government. I think this could stop elected officials from becoming career politicians and from perpetuating the power of the two-party system. It also might allow more third-party candidates to run and win.

Al Gore *(right)*, the Democratic nominee in the 2000 presidential election, listens while George W. Bush *(left)*, the Republican nominee, makes a point at a televised debate in North Carolina.

During his gubernatorial campaign, Ventura promised college students, "We're gonna shock the world" on Election Day.

Our best bet for the future is to get young people involved in the political process. An apathetic public is exactly what government enjoys best, but an interested public is what will make government work the best. Whatever criticisms I make of government and bureaucracy, the success of government ultimately comes back to the voters. Voting is both a privilege and a responsibility. People have given their lives to protect our right to vote. We owe it to ourselves and to each other to exercise that right.

"I KNEW...THAT IF I COULD REACH KIDS,...I HAD A GOOD CHANCE. SO I VISITED SCHOOLS AND WENT TO AREAS OF CITIES WHERE YOUNG PEOPLE HUNG OUT."

THE HISTORY OF SUFFRAGE

Although more than 100 million Americans can vote, voting—also known as suffrage—has not always been so easy in this country. In fact, when the United States first became a country, more people couldn't vote than could. Poor people couldn't vote. Neither could white women, Indians, black men and women, or anyone younger than twenty-one. This, of course, left only wealthy white men to vote. And it also left only wealthy white men to serve as president, senators, representatives, governors, and mayors.

Things changed, but slowly. Poor white men were the first to gain the vote in the 1820s, when the government did away with the property and income requirements. Black men got the right to vote after the Civil War, when the Fifteenth Amendment was passed in 1870.

Meanwhile, women struggled to gain their suffrage—and not silently. Women had long been pushing the federal government to change its view. In 1878, after almost thirty years of trying, a bill was finally introduced in Congress to give women the right to vote. It was defeated. The same bill was introduced in Congress each year for more than forty years. Black women and

Supporters of women's suffrage encourage a "yes" vote.

white women got the right to vote in 1920, when Congress and the states approved the Nineteenth Amendment.

Although things improved for white women, things did not get better for blacks. Even though they could legally vote, blacks were kept from voting in many southern states. In the 1890s, for example, many southern states had poll taxes. These were fees that people had to pay before being allowed to vote. The cost kept many blacks from voting.

Southern states also had literacy, or reading, tests that people had to pass before voting. Usually, blacks were given failing grades (and kept from voting),

In 1963 hundreds of thousands of people gathered in Washington, D.C., to support civil rights.

while whites were given passing grades so they could vote. It was not until the 1950s and 1960s, when Dr. Martin Luther King Jr. and others led protests against such practices, that the federal government passed more laws to guarantee the civil rights of blacks. The Twenty-fourth Amendment ended the use of poll taxes. And the 1965 Voting Rights Act did away with literacy tests all over the country.

The next big change in the voting laws happened in 1971, during the Vietnam War. Thousands of young people who were over the age of eighteen but under twenty-one had been drafted and sent to fight in Vietnam. These young draftees couldn't signal their opinion of the war by voting for president or for congressional leaders. This seemed unfair, so in 1971 the Twenty-sixth Amendment was passed. It lowered the voting age in the United States to eighteen.

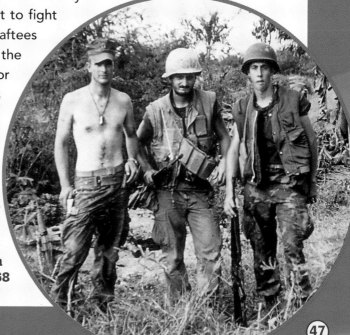

Young U.S. Marines in South Vietnam, 1968

5 CUTTING

HERE'S AN ANALOGY for you. Yeah, big word, but it basically means a comparison that highlights a point. Most people consider Egypt's Great Pyramid of Giza, because of its size, one of the wonders of the world. The mummified body of a guy named Pharaoh Khufu lies inside. Experts say the tomb took 100,000 workers about twenty years to construct. It's estimated the pyramid cost Khufu the equivalent of millions of dollars to build.

Getting financial approval for building an ancient pyramid was pretty easy. The process of approving and organizing the building of a modern highway can take a long time.

UP THE PIE

Perhaps the most amazing part is that Pharaoh Khufu didn't have to get anyone's permission to use Egypt's tax money for the pyramid's construction. He didn't have to discuss the project with any other government officials or even with his subjects. He simply ordered thousands of stonemasons and laborers to get movin'.

That's a far cry from how most governments operate today, especially in the United States, where spending people's money is an incredibly detailed process. This is true whether at the federal level—building interstate highways—or at the local level, such as putting in a soccer field.

All governments collect money in the form of taxes. Everything the government does costs money, so, in effect, taxes pay for everything. The school bus you ride was paid for with tax money. Even if your family gives you a lift, the roads you drive on were paid for by taxes. You say you walk to school. Well, even the sidewalks were paid for by tax dollars. Without taxes, local, state, and federal governments couldn't build a park or pay someone to counsel a troubled teenager or provide medical care to a low-income family. Thousands and thousands of workers in a huge variety of jobs—highway construction crews, state and national park guides, and some teachers, to name just a few—are on government payrolls.

Working teenagers have payroll taxes taken out of their paychecks. This money goes to the government.

It's not only adults or government officials who play a part in this whole process. Think back to the last time you were at the mall to buy a CD. You probably didn't realize that you were helping to keep the U.S. government operating. In fact, each time you

have a hamburger and fries with your friends at a fast-food restaurant or buy a new Play Station game, you are also doing your part to keep your city, state, and county governments running.

How? Because each time you buy something, you or your parents are paying sales taxes to the government. This is paid on top of the price the store or business charges for what you buy. The amount of sales tax is usually shown at the bottom of your receipt. It doesn't stop there. When kids are old enough to start working for wages, usually by the time they are fifteen or sixteen, money is taken from their pay as taxes and given to the government. These are called payroll taxes. The more you make, the more money is taken out.

Local and state governments regulate their own sales taxes, which are added to the subtotal of many purchases.

The money collected is put into a large pot called a general fund. Using this fund, the federal, state, and local governments then each make up a budget of the things that will be paid for and how much will be paid for them. Some items come up every year (such as paying for police officers and firefighters). They are paid for with money that always comes in. Some items (such as building a bridge or a school) only need to be paid for once, so these are usually paid for by special funds. Special funds are usually raised by taxing only the people who are going to use the facility or who live in the area that is going to benefit from the improvement.

All governments are bound by law to create a budget. Even though Congress, the state legislatures, and the city councils say how this money will be spent, all parts of the government get involved in setting up these priorities. That includes the court systems, because local and federal courts are often called upon to review a program. This review can result in a program being stopped, started, or changed.

SPECIAL-INTEREST GROUPS

The Society for the Preservation of Ice Cream and the No More Homework Coalition are not real groups, at least not yet. Although these goals might sound silly, there is nothing in the Constitution to stop such groups from forming to ask Congress, the president, or city council members to help preserve ice cream or stop homework. These groups, from the silly to the serious, are called special-interest groups, because they are very focused on one cause.

Members of thousands of special-interest groups walk the halls of Congress or state capitols trying to get the attention of officeholders. There are lobbying groups for animals, plants, birds, dairy farmers, automobile companies, teachers, and even grandparents.

To be a special-interest group, about all that is needed is to find people who believe in the same cause. Then a special-interest group registers with the state or federal government and lets it know what the group intends to do. Supporters collect money from members or sympathizers to publicize the cause or to fund the political campaigns of candidates who promise to vote the way the special-interest group wants.

One of the things that sets me apart from other politicians is my refusal to accept money from special-interest groups. Instead, I've taken out personal loans, and I only accept donations from individuals. I believe this allows me to speak my mind without worrying about whether I'll get further funding from supporters.

As a result, I can govern with no strings attached. People may disagree with my decisions. That's good. That's America. That's democracy. But one thing they can be assured of is that the decisions are mine and mine alone. Having no strings attached is so great that, if I run for reelection, I will promise the people of Minnesota that I will not actively raise a dime. The people of Minnesota will know my record. If they approve, they will reelect me. If not, they won't. Win or lose, my conscience will be clear.

In my view, special interests control our government today, point-blank, no doubt about it. They contribute vast amounts of money to the major parties for "party-building purposes." This cash doesn't come under the restrictions on contributions because it's not for a specific campaign. The parties can use this so-called soft money any way they see fit—on advertising, consultants, new water coolers, building rents, wall-to-wall carpeting, whatever.

Most of the money candidates spend comes from lobbyists. These people represent the special interests and give money to candidates in the hope of influencing their decisions. To me, as well as to other political observers, it seems like the candidates are selling themselves to the highest bidder. The result, observers say, is that candidates are not truly campaigning for what they believe in. Instead, they are sponsoring the positions of their biggest supporters. Campaign finance reform is the solution. The people need to wake up to the fact that, for the most part, their two major parties are manipulated by behind-the-scenes special-interest groups.

Demonstrators sit on the steps of the U.S. Capitol to protest Medicare vouchers. They represent a special-interest group of older women.

Running the government is so complex that it's almost impossible to predict exactly how much money is needed. At times, although not often, the government takes in more money than it needs in a given year. Sometimes the government gives some or all of the money back to the taxpayers by reducing the income tax, the sales tax, or the property tax. Other times, the government sends a check directly to the taxpayers. (Minnesotans got a sales tax rebate in 1999, 2000, and 2001. The federal government sent an income tax rebate in 2001.) Most often, the government keeps the extra money and puts it away in a reserve fund for future use or creates new programs that the tax money will pay for. Sometimes the government even pays off some of its debts.

A good way to understand how much people pay in taxes is by figuring out when Tax Freedom Day is each year. This imaginary day reflects when a taxpayer has worked enough in a year to pay all of his or her taxes for that year. The taxpayer can keep any money made after that day.

Here's an example. When the government began collecting income tax in 1913, Tax Freedom Day was on January

A girl supports her government by shopping.

30, meaning a taxpayer had to work for about one month to pay off the year's taxes. In 2000 Tax Freedom Day was May 3, meaning a taxpayer had to work more than four months to pay off the year's taxes.

This growth in the amount of taxes collected gave me an idea: do away with all income taxes and raise money only through sales taxes. I figured that the sales tax, which I call a consumption tax, would allow people the freedom to decide how much tax money they want to pay. If they don't mind paying a lot of taxes, they'll buy a lot of things no matter what their income level is. If they don't want to pay a lot of taxes, they'll keep their spending down. In my view, this idea gives more freedom to the taxpayer. It allows you to pay taxes by the lifestyle you live.

I believe this approach gets back to a more traditional interpretation of the Constitution, because it gives individuals more personal choice. People would enjoy more political freedom and economic benefits. That's the whole point of why taxes are paid and why the government spends so much time dividing up the pie.

PERSONAL FREEDOM

I think the Founding Fathers wanted to give a lot of freedom and responsibility to individuals. This means that people have the right to be smart and to do good things that will help themselves, their families, and their society. But at the same time, as long as people are willing to accept the responsibility and consequences of their actions, the government should leave them alone and not try to prevent them from doing foolish things to themselves or their lives.

I don't think you can make laws that'll stop people from doing stupid things. People are going to be stupid. That's part of our freedom. You have the freedom to be smart. And you have the freedom to be stupid, as long as you are not harming anyone else.

WHAT CAN

I'M ASKED JUST ABOUT EVERY DAY of the week to make a speech to some group or other. I've talked to journalists, businesspeople, politicians, and ordinary folks on farms and in cities and small towns across the country. But probably my most enjoyable and important talks have been with students. I say, keep talking to them, telling them the truth. Keep them involved.

I don't think it matters whether the kids are in elementary school, junior high, or high school. I pretty much tell them the same thing: that they are the future of democracy in the United States. I tell them that, regardless of their age, they must get involved if they want to improve the political system of the United States.

Let's go back to the 2000 election for president. What were the major topics? Social security and prescription drugs for the elderly. Well, what's going to inspire a young person to get involved over that? First of all, they're not going to see social security for many years. And most young people are pretty healthy. They're not worried about getting arthritis medicine.

The reason that those issues dominated this last election is that the elected officials know elderly people vote. They know that, to these old people, voting is their civic duty. These are people who can put a candidate in office, so the candidates are going to focus on them. Young people traditionally don't vote, so therefore politicians aren't going to pay attention to them.

> **Governor Ventura waves to an enthusiastic crowd of college students, urging them to vote in every election.**

KIDS DO

It might appear that there isn't much kids can do to affect politics in the United States of America. But I believe even young people in elementary and junior high have a part to play. Kids should not only be taught about government and politics at a fairly early age, say by the time they hit fourth grade, but they should then turn around and share what they have learned with their parents and other adults.

When I meet with kids, I always say, question the status quo, whether it be their teacher or whoever. I encourage them to ask their parents a lot of questions about politics and voting and what is going on in local government. Kids can help make sure parents are knowledgeable voters. They can share with parents what was learned in school. They can tell them they need to participate, because that's going to make life better for them.

In this way, the future of the United States will not only be protected but improved on. Adults will be forced to think about the issues and about voting, and hopefully young people will begin a lifelong connection to the voting process. All of which, I believe, will produce more informed voters in the future, which can only serve to produce better politicians and a better society.

Apathy is our biggest problem. I keep telling kids, you wanna become a player, you've gotta start voting. If you become a voting block, then politicians are going to pay attention to you. It's as simple as that.

In 2000 even nonvoting kids showed their spirit, as they voiced support for Al Gore *(above top)*, George W. Bush *(above middle)*, and Ralph Nader *(above bottom)*. Mock elections *(right)* also took place in many elementary schools across the country.

THE ELECTORAL COLLEGE

Although people in the United States may think they are voting directly for president when they cast their ballot, they are not. Instead, they are voting directly for electors. The electors then get to vote for the next president.

If the process sounds confusing, that's because it is. You can blame it all on the Founding Fathers, who created the electoral college because they couldn't agree on the best way to elect a president. Some delegates wanted a popular vote. (Under this system, whoever gets the most votes from eligible voters wins.) Others wanted Congress to select from among several candidates. The electoral college was seen as the best compromise, because it allowed the voters to be involved, but it was not a popular-vote system.

How are the electors finalized? By the voters. Each state has a specific number of electors, or electoral votes. This number equals the size of that state's congressional delegation—that is, its two senators plus however many representatives that state has in the House of Representatives. The more people who live in a state, the more representatives it has.

Each of the major parties puts forward a slate, or list, of people who pledge they'll vote for that party's candidate. When a voter votes for the Democratic Party's candidate, he or she is voting for the Democratic slate of electors.

The state's electoral votes usually have a winner-take-all format. That means the party slate that gets the most votes gets all of that state's electoral votes. Let's say the Republican slate for Massachusetts wins, then all of the state's twelve electoral votes go to the Republican candidate, regardless of whether the candidate wins by one vote or one million votes.

Under the electoral college system, a candidate can lose the popular vote across the country but still win the electoral vote and become president. This is exactly what happened in the 2000 race between George W. Bush and Al Gore. It was the fifth time in U.S. history that a candidate won the popular vote but lost the presidency. (The other times were in 1800, 1824, 1876, and 1888.) Personally, I believe in a popular vote.

There have been lots of attempts to abolish or reform the electoral college, but the smaller states have usually been able to defeat these proposals. The reason: if candidates only had to worry about winning the popular vote, they would spend all their time campaigning in the states with the largest populations. There would be no great reason for candidates to go to Wyoming, Rhode Island, or North Dakota. And candidates would have no incentive to work on the problems in those small states.

VENTURA'S IDEAS

I know I'm not your typical politician. So you might expect that my political and social ideas are out of the ordinary, too. Here's a sampling of my ideas.

★ **Merge the Minnesota house and senate to create a unicameral, or one-body, legislature.** I think a unicameral system would be the most effective method of getting things passed, because bills and discussions would not have to be duplicated by both a house and a senate. Some good ideas never see the light of day because of the effort it takes to get bills through the discussion process. Right now, out of our fifty states, only Nebraska has a unicameral legislature.

> "SOME GOOD IDEAS NEVER SEE THE LIGHT OF DAY BECAUSE OF THE EFFORT IT TAKES TO GET BILLS THROUGH THE DISCUSSION PROCESS."

★ **During a four-year term, spend one of those years discarding laws that are no longer useful to the state.** No new laws would be discussed that year.

★ **Refund budget surpluses.**

★ **Reform property taxes so that they don't go up if your property increases in value.**

★ **Lower business taxes.** This would allow companies to keep more of the money they make so they can develop their businesses and employ more workers.

★ **Attack crime by enforcing the laws on the books.** I think people should grit their teeth and support the death penalty, at least until such time as life in prison means life in prison and criminals are not allowed to leave prisons early.

FURTHER READING

Agel, Jerome, and Mort Gerberg. *The U.S. Constitution for Everyone.* New York: Perigree Books, 2001. This lively book details how the Founding Fathers argued and finally compromised to create one of America's most important documents.

Krull, Kathleen. *A Kid's Guide to America's Bill of Rights: Curfews, Censorship, and the 100-Pound Giant.* New York: Avon Books, Inc., 1999. This guide to the Bill of Rights gives an introductory description of what the Bill of Rights is and its purpose in America. It also describes how each bill affects people's daily lives.

Krull, Kathleen. *Lives of the Presidents: Fame, Shame (and What the Neighbors Thought).* New York: Raintree/Steck Vaughn, 1998. An insightful and entertaining overview of the lives of our presidents, the book focuses mainly on the human side of each president rather than on the historical facts.

Miller, Marilyn. *Words That Built a Nation: A Young Person's Collection of Historic American Documents.* New York: Scholastic, Inc., 1999. A collection of important documents, this book includes everything from the Constitution to Dr. Martin Luther King's famous "I Have a Dream" speech. The book accompanies every document with a short summary of why it is important and what its author intended to accomplish.

St. George, Judith. *So You Want to Be President?* New York: Philomel Books, 2000. Humorous and informative, this book is packed with fun facts about the presidents of the United States. It talks about everything from presidential pets to what the presidents served at their dinner tables.

West, Delno C., and Jean M. West. *Uncle Sam and Old Glory: Symbols of America.* New York: Atheneum Books for Young Readers, 2000. This book provides the basic history of some of the most important symbols of the United States, from the flag to Smokey Bear.

WEBSITES

Each state of the Union has an official website that uses a consistent format: <http://www.state.[your state's two-letter abbreviation].us.> For example, the website for Minnesota is <http://www.state.mn.us>.

AMERICA'S FREEDOM DOCUMENTS
<http://www.earlyamerica.com/earlyamerica/freedom/>
An archive site, America's Freedom Documents provides the original texts of the Declaration of Independence, the Bill of Rights, and the U.S. Constitution. The site also gives a brief history of each document and an explanation of what is important about it.

BEN'S GUIDE TO U.S. GOVERNMENT FOR KIDS
<http://www.bensguide.gpo.gov>
Follow Ben Franklin through the various levels of the U.S. government with this fun and interactive website. Divided into four age levels, the site provides information that kids of all ages can understand.

FIRSTGOV FOR KIDS
<http://www.kids.gov/k_gov.htm>
FirstGov for Kids is a great resource site that provides links to individual, state-maintained sites, as well as kid-friendly sites that deal with the U.S. government.

KIDS CORNER OF THE NATIONAL CONSTITUTION CENTER
<http://www.constitutioncenter.org/sections/kids/kids_main.asp>
This site gives information on a variety of aspects of government, including how to become a judge, and has fun activities for kids dealing with the Constitution.

WHITE HOUSE FOR KIDS
<http://www.whitehouse.gov/kids/>
This bright and colorful site has a tour of the White House as well as information on presidential pets and biographies of presidents and the vice presidents.

INDEX

ABOUT THE AUTHORS

Before becoming governor of Minnesota, **JESSE VENTURA** was a Navy SEAL, a professional wrestler, a television football commentator, a radio host, and a film star (*Predator* and *The Running Man*). He has written two previous books on politics, *I Ain't Got Time to Bleed*, a *New York Times* bestseller, and *Do I Stand Alone?* Governor Ventura lives in St. Paul, Minnesota, with his wife, son, and daughter.

HERÓN MÁRQUEZ has worked as a writer and editor for such newspapers as the New York *Daily News*, the *Los Angeles Times*, and the Minneapolis *Star Tribune*. He has written a number of books for young readers, including *George W. Bush*. Márquez lives in St. Paul, Minnesota, with his wife.

PHOTO ACKNOWLEDGMENTS

Photos used in this book are reproduced courtesy of: Eric Saulitis/Stafford Photography, Minneapolis, MN, pp. 2, 8, 26, 30, 41, 52, 60; © CORBIS, p. 6; © STAR TRIBUNE/Minneapolis-St. Paul, pp. 7, 9, 10, 13 (bottom), 42, 45; © Ventura For Minnesota, Inc., p. 11; © Jim West, pp. 12, 23 (bottom), 43, 48-49, 50, 58 (all); © Reuters/Scott Cohen/Hulton Archive, p. 13 (top); © Paul Almasy/CORBIS, p. 15; © MPI/Hulton Archive, p. 16; © Carmen Redondo/CORBIS, p. 17; © The Virginia Museum of Fine Arts, Gift of Colonel and Mrs. Edgar W. Garbisch, pp. 18–19; © Joseph Sohm; Visions of America/CORBIS, p. 20; Library of Congress, pp. 21 (LC-USZC4-2541), 27 (LC-USZC4-2528), 46 (LC-USZ62-7090); Independent Picture Service, pp. 22, 25, 29; Coalition to Stop Gun Violence, p. 23 (top); © Reuters NewMedia, Inc./CORBIS, p. 28; © AP/Wide World Photos, pp. 31, 32, 34, 35, 39, 40, 53; © AFP/CORBIS, pp. 33, 37, 44; The Supreme Court Historical Society, p. 36 (top); © Adam Woolfitt/CORBIS, p. 36 (bottom); U.S. Department of Defense, p. 38; National Archives, p. 47 (top); © Guido Alberto Rossi/Hulton Archive, p. 47 (bottom); © Bettmann/CORBIS, p. 48 (top); © Todd Strand/Independent Service, p. 51; © Tony Arruza/CORBIS, p. 54; © Jason Wachter/St. Cloud Times, p. 57.

Cover photo by Eric Saulitis/Stafford Photography, Minneapolis, MN.